GHOST MUS

Peter Martin was born in 1944 in Staffordshire. He trained for a career in education and taught at schools in West Sussex and Suffolk and at an adventure training centre in Scotland. When a childhood interest in natural history re-emerged, he left teaching to embark on a long career with environmental organisations - firstly with RSPB in South East England and then with WWF–UK, nationally and internationally. Latterly he was Chief Officer of the South Downs Society. He is now retired and lives with his wife in Seaford.

His first collection of poems, *'Seasons Regained'*, was published by Publish America in 2005.

The artist **H.H. Evans** was born in Seaford in 1849 and died in 1926. His great grandfather had been the vicar of St Leonard's, Seaford's parish church; his father was a surgeon and also a magistrate and Freeman of Seaford. H.H. Evans had only one arm, but when and how he lost his arm is unknown, as is his means of income, other than a period as an office clerk.

Much of his output is based on or copied from drawings, paintings or photographs and he produced many sets of drawings which he sold; rumour has it that he would also exchange them for drinks at the bar of The Plough public house.

He seems to have spent his whole life in Seaford and was buried in Seaford Cemetery.

ACKNOWLEDGEMENTS

I am grateful to:

My mother, Ruth Mountford, for moving to Seaford in 1967;

The staff of the Seaford Museum and Heritage Society and The Sussex Archaeological Society for their help in accessing information and for permission to use the map and illustrations which appear within the book;

Patricia Martin for her critical first reading of the poems and her careful and sympathetic editing of the manuscript at its many and various stages;

Tom Cunliffe for his invaluable help in the preparation of a print-ready manuscript and for creating the book cover.

GHOST MUSIC

POETRY AND HISTORY OF SEAFORD AND THE CUCKMERE VALLEY

Peter Martin

Illustrations: H.H. Evans 1849 – 1926

Seacroft Arts

First published in 2010
by Seacroft Arts, Seaford, East Sussex
redfox.martin@btinternet.com

Printed and bound in Great Britain by
CPI Antony Rowe, Chippenham and Eastbourne

All rights reserved

Text copyright Peter Martin
Front cover drawing and the drawing that appears on page 8 copyright
Seaford Museum and Heritage Society
The map and all other drawings copyright The Sussex Archaeological Society

No part of this book may be reproduced, stored in a retrieval system or transmitted in any form or by any means without the prior permission of the author or copyright holders, except by a reviewer who may quote brief passages in a printed review.

ISBN 978-0-9564540-0-3

DEDICATION

To my wife Patricia who sadly is unable to join me on my walks, but who has given unfailing inspiration and encouragement to this project.

The poem 'Hope Beach' is dedicated to our grandsons, Justin and Aaron.

CONTENTS

COMMON GROUND
- **The People** — 1
- **Churches** — 5
- **Rural Poor and Smuggling** — 7

SEAFORD TOWN
- **History** — 13
- **The Poems**

Celebrating All Souls — 23
Seaford Harbour — 27
Ghost Music — 30
The Hottest Day — 31
Doom Crows — 33
Sea-watching — 34

SEAFORD HEAD
- **Natural History** — 37
- **The Poems**

Splash Point — 45
Sea Pinks — 47
The Apothecary's Garden — 49
The Poisoner's Gift — 50
Lost in Transit — 51
Venus and a New Moon — 52
Easter Sonnet — 53
Spring Pictures — 54
Hope Beach — 55

CUCKMERE VILLAGES
- **History** — 57
- **The Poems**

Cuckmere Hauntings — 65

Poynings Town	66
A Day by the Sea 1919	68
Golden Ages	70
Garden Party	72
Corelli on the Tye	73
The Smallest Church	74
Sundial at Litlington Church	77
Fireside Thoughts	79
Westdean	81
The Last Oxen	83
Exceat	84

THE CUCKMERE VALLEY
- **Natural History** — 87
- **The Poems**

Seven Sisters	97
Folk Song	98
Colours of November	100
Cuckmere Illusions	101
The Cusp of the Seasons	102
On the Edge of Things	104
Of Magpies and Rainbows	105
Homecoming	106
Waiting	107
Old May Day	109
Glow Worms	110
Winter Solstice	111
Under Haven Brow	112

EPILOGUE — 114

BIBLIOGRAPHY — 116

PREFACE

Seaford and the Cuckmere valley have been studied extensively and there are many excellent and detailed publications describing the human and natural histories that have shaped the character of this part of East Sussex.

However, landscapes and places have a presence that goes beyond the factual – something that is experienced through all our senses, our imaginations and, for many people, another dimension that is in the realm of the emotions or spirituality.

This book combines these very different aspects of the environment in a mixture of prose and poetry. Both have been informed by a wealth of written material and stimulated by a series of walks and visits to places between Seaford, Seaford Head, Hope Gap, Cuckmere Haven and then following the Cuckmere river upstream to Alfriston; from there, heading back towards the sea via the villages of Lullington, Litlington, Westdean and the lost village of Exceat, and ending or beginning on the beach under Haven Brow, the highest and most westerly of the Seven Sisters.

Seaford and the Cuckmere valley from a map dated 1808

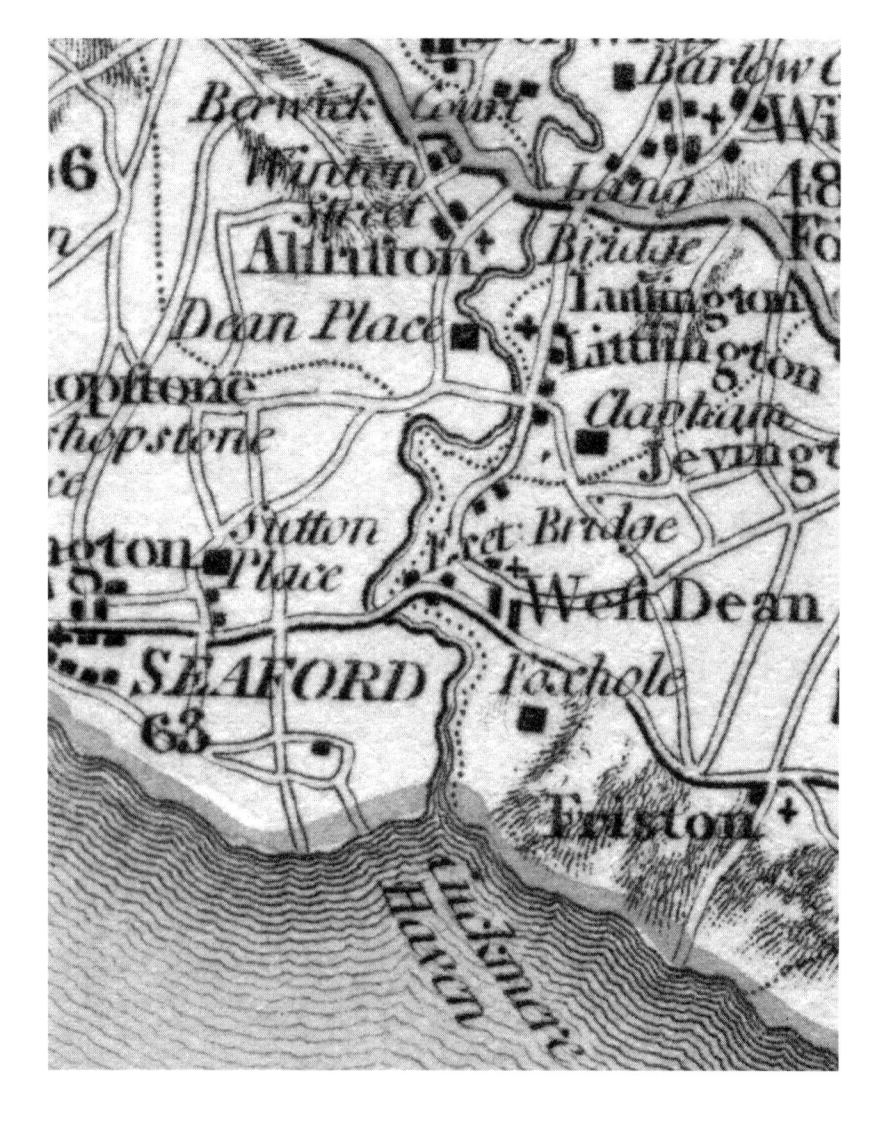

THE PEOPLE

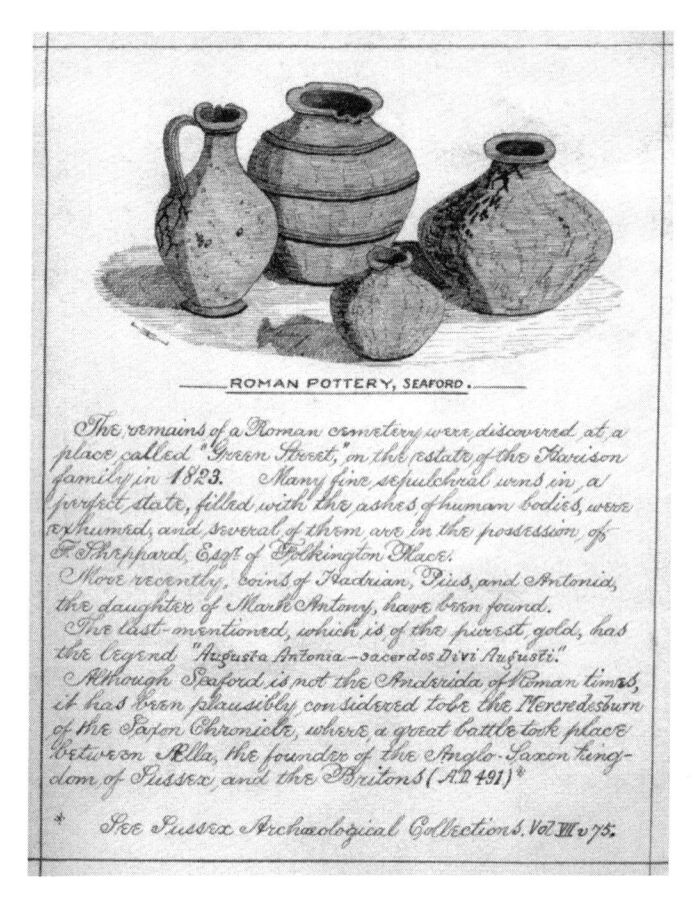

Roman Pottery found at Seaford in 1823

The remains of a Roman cemetery were discovered at a place called "Green Street," on the estate of the Harison family in 1823. Many fine sepulchral urns, in a perfect state, filled with the ashes of human bodies, were exhumed, and several of them are in the possession of R. Shephard, Esq? of Folkington Place.

More recently, coins of Hadrian, Pius, and Antonia, the daughter of Mark Antony, have been found. The last-mentioned, which is of the purest gold, has the legend "Augusta Antonia—sacerdos Divi Augusti." Although Seaford is not the Andrida of Roman times, it has been plausibly considered to be the Mercredesburn of the Saxon Chronicle, where a great battle took place between Ælla, the founder of the Anglo-Saxon kingdom of Sussex, and the Britons (A.D. 491)*

* *See Sussex Archaeological Collections. Vol VII v 75.*

Hundreds of thousands of years ago the coastlines of southern Britain were joined to mainland Europe. Prehistoric nomadic hunters and gatherers followed herds of game across this landmass killing and butchering wild horses and deer with flint weapons and tools. The first evidence of this dates from 500,000 years ago and was unearthed at Boxgrove in West Sussex.

Sometime later, thought to be around 400,000 years ago, water broke through the land bridge and scoured a deep flooded valley, creating what is now the English Channel. However, it was not until 180,000 years ago that Britain's break from the rest of Europe was fully completed.

Nomadic hunters no doubt continued to hunt across Britain as and when conditions allowed, but it was not until the climate was free of the impact of glaciers that continuous habitation was possible. The earliest evidence of human occupation in the Seaford area includes Stone Age flint implements, such as hand axes, dating from over 8,000 years ago.

Around 4-5,000 BC more sophisticated land management skills arrived in north-west Europe with the New Stone Age or Neolithic people. They used stone and bone tools to clear trees from the Downs in order to cultivate crops, graze livestock and thus develop a more settled way of life. More advanced technologies such as working bronze around 2,000 BC and iron around 800 BC, plus skills such as spinning, weaving and making pottery, contributed to the evolution of community living within a functioning arable and pastoral landscape. Not only did these people leave a lasting legacy of open downland, they also left evidence of their defensive earthworks, field boundaries and burial mounds, known as barrows, across the Downs.

These were not a unified people but a collection of tribes originating from across mainland Europe, so when the Romans arrived in 43 BC they found a number of named Celtic peoples but little sign of any collective 'British' identity.

The Roman occupation, which lasted until 409 AD, was in the main a military presence, consisting of army personnel, administrators and small numbers of traders. It is estimated that in total these made up only 3% of the small, 3 million or so, population but they provided vital protection against any other aggressive forces; this included the building of forts along the south coast of England to combat the ever-present threat of Saxon raids. Where the Romans dominated, which included much of modern-day England, a Romano-British identity evolved, even though Celtic, with little Latin influence, remained the language of the general population. However, when the Roman Empire declined the imperial armies withdrew and the Romano-British power structures and defences began to collapse; this left little protection against full scale invasion and colonisation by Jutes, Angles and Saxons from the near Continent.

Over time four separate Anglo-Saxon kingdoms evolved, Wessex, East Anglia, Mercia and Northumbria – inhabited by people who spoke various dialects of a Germanic language. The Celts were enslaved, slaughtered or found refuge in Cornwall, Wales and Scotland; their language and culture had little or no influence on the Anglo-Saxons or on the evolution of what would become a distinctive Anglo-Saxon culture and eventually, an English language.

It was not until 465 that Saxons from the North German plain are thought to have landed in Sussex and, under the leadership of Aelle, defeated a Romano-British army on the banks of a small river, which may have been the Cuckmere. They created the small kingdom of Sussex, the land of the South Saxons, but it was too small to be viable and ultimately was absorbed into the larger kingdom of Wessex.

Wessex was to become of major importance to the Anglo-Saxons, for when the Vikings invaded the kingdoms of East Anglia, Northumbria and parts of Mercia, Wessex remained a stronghold for both the Anglo-Saxon people and their language. Alfred, King of Wessex from 871 to 899, managed to unite the kingdoms of Wessex and Mercia, and by successful military achievements and shrewd treaties with the Vikings, laid the foundations for the Anglo-Saxons to regain control. This was finally achieved by his grandson Athelstan; following a decisive victory over the Vikings in 937 he was able to create a united kingdom of England with a unifying spoken and written English language. The Vikings re-invaded in 1014 and

Canute became king in 1016, although the throne returned to the Anglo-Saxons with Edward the Confessor in 1042.

The 600 or so years of Saxon and Viking rule ended in 1066 with the Norman invasion and England became an adjunct to the Normans' land in France. The governing, land-owning and military elite subjugated the Anglo-Saxon people with considerable brutality, but although French became the language of royalty and state, English remained the language of the populace. However, with voluntary or forced interaction, including intermarriage, the Anglo-Saxons began to integrate French words into their vocabulary.

French-born, French-speaking Kings, who often spent little time in England, continued to rule. However, by 1206 King John had lost most of his land in France to the French King and the Normans in England became alienated from their homeland; France then became the enemy and years of territorial conflicts ensued. This was of great significance to Seaford and the Cuckmere valley villages as they suffered badly from French attacks, especially during the '100 Years War' from 1337 to 1453.

The English language, enriched by French, became a unifying force across society and by the 1360s it emerged as the language of business and government and finally, by the end of the century, of royalty.

CHURCHES

Westdean Church

Christianity was brought to England in the 2nd century by traders from the eastern Mediterranean and from the late 4th century it was the state religion of the Roman Empire. When the Romans left Britain, large parts of the country were colonised by pagan invaders and Christianity died out almost completely. Missionaries from mainland Europe supported any remaining believers but this was fraught with danger; in the 6th century, a Sussex woman, Lewinna, was martyred for her faith and was later made a saint. The details of her death and the whereabouts of her final burial place are uncertain, although Alfriston lays tentative claim to this due to the presence of a small carving of her face in St Andrew's Church. It was not until the 7th century that St. Wilfred converted the South Saxons to Christianity and open Christian worship became possible.

Once the faith became established, missionaries set up stone crosses to mark where worship would take place; over time these open-air churches were replaced by buildings, with larger churches or minsters housing monks, priests and nuns who served outlying areas. Later, smaller churches were built by local Lords for their families, tenants and serfs and this formed the basis of a parish system. Many Sussex churches originated at this time, some of which were built on the site of pagan temples thereby maintaining traditional places of worship. The timing of many Christian festivals was also chosen to coincide with traditional pagan celebrations so that pagan beliefs, Christianity, myth and folklore intermingled.

Saxon buildings were typically constructed from wood, wattle, daub and thatch but even before the Norman invasion, stonemasons from Normandy influenced building in southeast England and churches often included more durable stone. Over the three hundred years after 1066 these buildings were augmented or fully replaced by stone structures and the wonderful South Downs' churches came into being. They became a centre for parish life as whole communities participated in Sunday worship and in the many festivals and saints' days of the church calendar.

Many of these churches have retained much of their original simplicity of design and structure as, due to rural poverty and shrinking populations, they were not subjected to 17th century Gothic and 19th century Victorian enlargements and embellishments. Seaford's parish church of St Leonard is an exception. Here a large cruciform building was completed in 1090 and as the town and port grew in importance and size, the church was enlarged in 1120 and again in 1200. However, the decline of the town's fortunes in the 14th and 15th centuries saw the church slip into disrepair with part of it being burned down by French raiders. In 1485 it was restored and a tower was added, but it was not until the more buoyant times of the mid 19th century that a major rebuild and restoration took place and the church took on its current size and shape.

RURAL POOR AND SMUGGLING

Alfriston Market Cross

Life was physically hard for South Downs' communities and to make matters worse they were subjected to taxes on traded goods and on their produce. Taxes were introduced in England during the Roman occupation and after the Romans left, Saxon Kings levied taxes on land and property. Later a tax was imposed on wine arriving at Billingsgate, requiring importers to give up a proportion of their cargo in return for permission to trade. This became the 'custom' to do so, hence the name. Taxes were used and abused by subsequent monarchs to fund both lavish lifestyles and territorial conflicts at home and abroad, often causing major social unrest such as the Peasants' Revolt of 1381. But it was not only royalty that extorted money from the people.

In 855 the Church had been granted the right to levy Tithes - one tenth of the parishioners' produce. These comprised the Great Tithe, levied on major items such as cattle and crops, and the Lesser Tithe that included everything else the village produced such as eggs, vegetables and fruit. In 1285 the levying of tithes became law, justified by the notion that it would make the peasants farm more efficiently.

Before the enclosure of common land, which took place between the 16th and 18th centuries, the rural labourers had a level of self-sufficiency, able to grow food and graze animals either on the common lands that were 'un-owned' or on owned land on which they had commoners' rights. Once these rights were progressively removed, the landless labourers became totally dependent on employment provided by landowners, tenant farmers or local industries. Agricultural and domestic labourers were recruited at hiring fairs where prospective employers and employees would gather and agree year-long contracts – in some places this tradition continued until the beginning of the 20th century. Those left unemployed became day-labourers and thus suffered from the vagaries of the weather and from any changes in farming methods. As a result, many died in the famines of the 1590s, 1620s and 1640s. Many more lost homes and became paupers and vagabonds, suffering appalling treatment when press-ganged into the Navy or when transported to the new colonies, effectively as slaves.

Even if they managed to find work and housing, the rural poor were also very vulnerable to any changes in the price of basic food, especially bread. During the Napoleonic Wars from 1793 to 1815, the landowners had no competition from overseas and were able to set high prices for their grain, so the price of bread was high. When the wars ended, the powerful landowners pressurised the Government into passing the Corn Laws to protect the price of UK corn so that foreign imports could not undercut the price set by UK producers, and bread remained expensive. Any attempt to live off the land by poaching was dealt with severely, man-traps were set and the death penalty was commonplace for such minor transgressions as stealing a rabbit.

This poverty and hardship periodically led to unrest and there were regular bread riots, notably after the severe winters of 1794 and 95. However, when machines began to replace what had been labour-intensive, manual jobs, the unrest became more violent. In the north of England the Luddite Rebellion of 1811 and 1812 aimed to destroy new machinery that replaced cottage workers in the textile industry, but a more widespread response was focussed in rural areas, especially in Sussex and Kent.

This came to a head with the invention of the threshing machine, first used in Sussex in 1810, which had a disastrous effect on agricultural labourers as it removed their traditional winter occupation. The powerless, alienated, hungry and, in many cases, destitute labourers wanted revenge and in the latter part of 1830 they set about breaking farm machinery and setting fire to barns, hay-ricks and even farm houses. This campaign of violence was accompanied by intimidating letters sent to the farmers signed by a probably non-existent 'Captain Swing'; thus they became known as the 'Swing Riots'.

However, for many years the people of Seaford and the Cuckmere valley had used a more direct and productive way of augmenting meagre wages and avoiding punitive taxation by church and state. In 1275, Edward I sought new revenues by imposing customs on wool exports and appointing officers to police compliance. The rise of wool smuggling or 'owling', a corruption of 'wooling', soon followed and over the years Alfriston in particular became a centre for this illicit trade. It was a two-way enterprise, with downland wool shipped to the continent and goods that attracted high import taxes, such as tea, lace, wine, spirits and tobacco, brought back to Sussex. The village was ideally suited as Cuckmere Haven provided an isolated landing beach with both river and track-way access inland and plenty of storage and hiding places in barns or cellars. Alternatively, there were many inaccessible beaches under the cliffs of Seaford Head and the Seven Sisters where cargo could be landed, then winched up the cliffs using mobile wooden 'derricks' with horse-driven windlasses or winches. A more dangerous method was for the cargo to be manhandled up the cliffs using rope ladders.

Coastguard Station and Cuckmere Haven

Smuggling soon become commonplace, especially as it was not until the 14th century that revenue cutters were employed around the coast to enforce legislation. This did not deter participation as the large rewards were worth any risk, particularly as the smugglers were often armed and could outnumber and beat off enforcement officers. However, such a lucrative business attracted severe penalties such as transportation and hanging and thus the smugglers often resorted to violence to avoid capture. By the mid 17th century the Sussex wool smugglers had developed a reputation for savagery; any captured revenue officers could be severely beaten or even killed and any locals who sided with the law were punished by beatings or damage to their property.

Smuggling reached its heyday in the late 18th and early 19th centuries with large organised gangs operating virtually unhindered by the law. In the 18th century a farm labourer earned no more than 30 pence for a six-day week and could earn up to 50 pence for a night's work with the smugglers. Also, as there was a general dislike of the taxes, the smugglers could count on large numbers of people from all levels of society to help unload cargo and transport it inland or to provide horses or storage places for the goods. Even if people did not play an active part, few could resist the offer of cheap luxury goods, some even placing special orders for particular products; others chose to keep quiet as they were fearful of reprisals. Large-scale smuggling continued until the mid 1880's, although it was hampered by the barracking of soldiers on both sides of Cuckmere Haven during the Napoleonic Wars and by the building and manning of coastguard stations at Cuckmere Haven (1809), Crowlink (1830s) and Birling Gap (1876).

SEAFORD TOWN

Seaford Beach Looking West 1897

Seaford is situated at the eastern end of a wide bay that faces south-west and thus straight into the prevailing winds and storms that sweep up the English Channel; this has had a significant impact on the growth and development of the town. The community was originally situated on a river estuary, bounded on the seaward side by a shingle spit that created a well protected natural harbour. One can safely assume that the river had a very wide area of intertidal mudflats, salt marshes and riverine woodland providing year-round sources of animal and plant food, materials for building and thatching and salt from the evaporation of seawater. In addition, the trees on the thin soil of the surrounding low chalk hills were easily cleared, producing timber for building, for fuel and to create fields for crop growing and stock-grazing.

Evidence of early occupation is provided by Bronze Age pottery found at Chyngton and remnants of a Bronze and Iron Age hill fort are still visible at Seaford Head, although most of these earthworks have long since fallen into the sea. The Romans possibly utilised this strategically sited fort for a camp of their own, although it is likely that this was soon abandoned. However, the discovery of a Roman burial ground, now obliterated by Seaford Head golf course, plus pottery and other artefacts indicates that Seaford continued to be occupied during the Roman period. In 1950 the bones of a young girl were found under Seaford Head and, as the skeleton was found to be of ancient origin, she was called the 'Roman Princess'; later research proved that the bones belonged to the next wave of colonisers, the Saxons.

In the early Middle Ages, what is now Seaford included the four separate communities of Seaford, Blatchington, Sutton and Chyngton. These were fishing and farming communities with Seaford having the added benefit of direct access to the sea. By the early 13th century Seaford was one of the busiest of the Channel ports, exporting wool from the flocks of downland sheep and importing wines. By the end of the 13th century there were 16 wool merchants listed for the port and Seaford's prosperity grew. As well as a bustling trading centre, Seaford was home to all the other supporting trades and services such as shipwrights, carpenters, chandlers, warehouse workers, blacksmiths, armourers plus fishermen, bakers, clothiers and inn-keepers.

The town was also of military importance. The Normans created a network of ports to provide ships and men for a national fleet. Seaford was one of these and was linked with Hastings, given the title of 'Ancient Town and Port' and gained a range of trading benefits; in 1298 it received the constitutional privilege of sending two members to Parliament.

But a mixture of natural and human causes meant that Seaford's prosperity and status did not last. The evolution of the powerful English and French nations led to many territorial conflicts with our nearest continental neighbours and regular damaging raids on the Sussex coast took place, in particular during the 100 Years War that began in 1338.

Seaford suffered badly, but worse followed when during 1348 and 1349 the Black Death ravaged the country and the population was drastically reduced. By 1356 Seaford's harbour was also in decline due to siltation and the constant movement of shingle which blocked the harbour mouth. Although the harbour could still accommodate small ships, this once prosperous and influential port become a part derelict township and had to relinquish its right to send MPs to Parliament. Sutton and Chyngton were similarly affected - Chyngton virtually disappeared and in 1509 both merged with Seaford, although this did not happen physically until extensive house-building took place in the 20th century.

Any chance of reclaiming Seaford's maritime glory disappeared in 1579 when the river Ouse was diverted to reach the sea at the western end of the bay. This was not to create a new harbour - that came later - but to ensure that Lewes and other riverside communities could reach the sea by boat without the problems created by the shallow and frequently blocked river mouth at Seaford. Following the harbour's demise, the town gained a less savoury reputation for smuggling and wrecking that enhanced the meagre income from fishing and farming.

In the 16th century there was some improvement in the town's fortunes - it received a Charter of Incorporation as a Cinque Port from Henry VIII, in 1544 it was confirmed as a Town, Borough and Parish and in 1641 it recovered the right to send members to Parliament. However, this was carried out in a less than democratic way. Seaford was a 'Rotten Borough' - a borough with a small population where the landowners and other wealthy members of the community could arrange for the election of carefully chosen candidates. The Reform Act of 1832 outlawed this process and Seaford, along with 57 other Rotten Boroughs, was disenfranchised.

Even after regular French raids decreased, the last recorded being in 1545, the Sussex coast remained in the front line when French invasion threatened. During the Napoleonic Wars from

1793 to 1815, a string of Martello Towers was built along the south coast of England - the well-preserved tower on Seaford's promenade is a relic of this defensive response, although it never saw active service.

Some 120 years later during the 2nd World War, the Sussex coast was once again in the front line of any potential invasion. Seaford became a restricted area, schools were closed and relocated and civilians were evacuated. Barbed wire was spread across the esplanade, the beach was mined and tank traps and gun emplacements built. Cuckmere Haven was similarly defended and lights were also rigged up in the lower part of the Cuckmere valley to deceive German bombers into attacking uninhabited farmland rather than Seaford or Newhaven. Despite these precautions, Seaford was attacked 42 times, 82 properties were destroyed or seriously damaged and 23 people were killed.

Over the centuries all the small coastal towns and fishing villages of Sussex suffered from periodic economic decline. However, in 1752 Dr Richard Russell asserted the restorative benefits of sea bathing and the Sussex coast, being close to London, was an attractive destination for wealthy patrons wishing to ease the many health problems of the 18th century. Visits to Brighton by the Prince Regent, later George IV, in 1783 and his subsequent development of the elaborate Brighton Pavilion as a seaside home provided considerable impetus to the growing popularity of seaside living. Eastbourne's growth was delayed until the railway arrived in 1849 which was followed by the Duke of Devonshire's sponsorship of a major development to create a resort 'built by gentlemen for gentlemen'.

Seaford's progress was far less dramatic as it did not have the necessary facilities to attract the clientele or wealthy benefactors to underwrite its development. It was not until 1840 that four boarding houses were opened but one visitor described Seaford, albeit in a lightly disguised short story, as characterised by 'shavenness, featureless, emptiness, clamminess, scurfiness and whiffs of sewage'.

Soon after, the Seaford Improvement Committee was set up to provide seats for visitors, plant tamarisk on the green, improve the beach, lay out walks and provide more bathing machines. However, its main achievement was to persuade the London and Brighton and South Coast Railway Company to build a branch line to Seaford, opened with due ceremony in 1864.

The Great Flood 1875

The Terminus Hotel was built close to the station and other improvements to the town soon followed, including the building of a gas works, improved drainage, installation of piped water and the construction of substantial residences.

Various projects were put forward to improve the town as a tourist destination and health resort. This was a challenging ambition, made even more so in 1875 when the town suffered a major flooding disaster. Severe storms breached the sea wall, low-lying land that was once the harbour was inundated and many properties were damaged. This led to the rebuilding and strengthening of the sea wall which, when completed in 1881, encouraged another spate of grand plans for the town. Most never materialised, including a proposed 450 yard long promenade pier with a jetty and landing places for passengers and goods, and later a less ambitious plan for a pier and jetty with refreshment rooms.

Wreck of the S.S. Gannet 1882

Other plans did get off the drawing-board. In 1886 the Seaford Bay Estate Company proposed a major building programme to create a grand residential development on and behind the seafront - along the lines of Brighton's Regency Squares. Winter gales delayed building and deterred would-be buyers. The Esplanade Hotel was the only prestigious building that was completed and, with few residential properties being built, the Company went bankrupt. In 1887 the Seaford Golf Course was opened on Seaford Head. This attracted some visitors, but there was little else for holidaymakers to do and the autumn and winter storms deterred year-round demand for accommodation. Ultimately most of the hotels closed down.

Seaford's bracing weather was not an entirely negative attribute as the town developed a reputation as a health spa, especially for those with lung complaints, and England's first Seaside Convalescent Home was opened in 1860. Others followed, providing employment for a range of professions and service providers. This healthy image and lack of distractions also attracted educationalists to Seaford and from the late 19th century to the middle of the 20th, private schools formed Seaford's main 'industry'. During this period, Seaford boasted around 50 private schools, although not all operated at the same time, some were very short-lived and few now remain.

The two World Wars halted any major development of the town. Since then plans of varying levels of ambition have been put forward and some implemented including the complete rebuilding of the beach. The sea wall formed the promenade and provided some protection from storm-driven waves that sometimes reached a height of over 15 metres; but this regular battering caused structural damage to both the sea wall and to seafront properties – some of which had to be demolished. Drastic solutions were sought and in 1987 a massive shingle beach 2500 metres long and 115 metres wide was created using 3 million tonnes of shingle obtained from the offshore sea bed. Although the beach is now usable even at high tide, Seaford remains less popular and populous than nearby Eastbourne and Brighton. Many local people prefer it that way and as a place to live it is much loved. It retains a 'village' feel, typified by its range of small shops, the climate, in spite of the storms, is benign and the new beach, backed by pastel-coloured beach huts, is attractive, peaceful and well-used, even though there is a constant battle to counteract the sea's determined realignment of the shore.

Seaford can be celebrated as a small friendly town with a proud and fascinating history and set in a very special and privileged position, bordered by the sea, virtually encircled by open downland and with the iconic cliffs of the Seven Sisters and the beautiful Cuckmere valley on its doorstep. These are some of the most visited, filmed, photographed and painted landscapes in England and are the most easily recognisable sections of the South Downs. On November 12th 2009, these chalk hills, stretching from Eastbourne to Winchester, were officially designated as the core of a new National Park; this status provides enhanced protection against damaging developments to 632 square miles of downland, woodland, wetland, farmland, heathland, villages and market towns in East Sussex, West Sussex and Hampshire.

SEAFORD TOWN

THE POEMS

Clinton Place and St Leonard's Church 1870

Celebrating All Souls

Why do I walk
The long way round
Under the lychgate
Into hallowed ground,
By the flint-flecked church
With no elegant spire,
Just squat and solid
As the proximate sea requires?

Is it the starlings'
Leaf-spinning dashes
Around the golden vane
The evening sun catches,
Or the drifting hawk
That lifts on the wind,
Slipping and tipping
On unsteady woodland wings?

Maybe the untruthful roses
Still summer-bright,
Unsullied petals
Fresh, pink and white,
Or the honest sycamore,
Leaves spent and falling
Urged by the wind into
Careless patterning?

Well yes and no,
The kaleidoscope reassures
In this place of stillness,
The vitality secures
The temporary
As an antidote
To the fickleness
Of this earth's rich memory.

Androgynous angels
Guard anonymous graves;
Those with no status and those
Whose epitaphs crave remembrance,
All level in the ground
And levelled by the sea-wind's
Scouring of the stone
And the communal mind.

In forgotten corners
Lost in a wreck of leaves,
Shaded by sycamore shrouds,
Draped in ivy's widow weeds
They lie neglected;
Someone's husband or wife,
Concealed testimonies
To the littleness of life.

So, as I tread
This tightrope path
With the other weather-blown and
Season-shifted chaff,
I dare to interfere,
To delve
And ask, 'who are you,
What of yourselves?'

I could be fanciful
And hear the mewling gulls
As responding voices
Telling stories full of answers;
But their purposes
Are too mundane
And their yellow eyes
Too profane

To give a voice to Sarah;

Sarah so elusive,
Even though the irises
On her grave are effusive
With brick-red seeds
And elegant leaves frame
The incised shadows
Of another's name.

Did you share so much
In life to wish the same in death?
Were you and Jane so close
To feel each other's breath
As long dresses brushed
The spin-drift sprayed
And wind-flayed shingle
Of a seaside promenade?

Maybe in the stone-chill church
There were hymns you sang
To the antique sound
Of a West Gallery band
Of bass-viol, clarionet,
Oboe and flute,
Until the decorous organ
Rendered quaintness mute.

And for this place
Of sixteen hundred souls
Alfred, the young policeman
Maintained control;
No doubt made easy
By the worthies of the town,
The bailiff, the mayor and those
Whose wealth bought renown.

But they could not keep him
From an early grave.

If his daughters, his son
And Mary his wife waved
That March morning
With salt in their eyes
From a wind-whipped sea,
It was a final goodbye.

Then, when swifts disappeared
Into mystic space,
James forsook his world
For another unfathomed place;
And Joseph, so respected
As he plied his surgeon's trade,
Could not with all his practiced skills
Avoid death's sharper blade.

Such sadness in the stones,
Such hardships would come,
Such anguish chiselled
In 'Thy will be done'.
So read the faded names
And briefly cryptic stories
To invoke those who lived long since
And celebrate their memories.

Seaford Harbour

Rebellious seas
Ordain destinies;
Spring tides and westerly winds
Create fickle histories
Of lasting significance.
Smell the mud and seaweed drying,
See the whistling wigeon flying,
Hear the curlew's wild-soul crying
And a sinking tide's soft sift sighing.

High prows and sterns
Of Galleys and castled Cogs
Round the headland,
Sails furled as rowers turn
For harbour.
Voyages ending as beginning,
Across the bar as the tide is turning,
People on the quayside waiting
With trepidation or hearts elating.

Green ways or chalk tracks
Lead to rest hard-earned
And bring mixed news
Of family lost, friends returned
And tales of a world beyond.
Grain and wool from chalk-down leas
Exchanged for brandy, spices, teas,
And well-fed merchants rest at ease
In inns where ale and stories please;

Recalling customs foiled
And battles won
When Calais was 'sieged
Or the enemy fleet undone
At Lespangnols-sur-mer.

Black Death's rampage,
The French fleet's raids,
A fire that purged and left no trade,
And a haven made was then un-made.

A sullen flowing river
Heavy with usurping clay
And sea-shifted shingle
Clattering around the bay
Rearrange the future.
Fishermen launch from shelving moorings
To seek out plaice, sprats and whiting,
Mackerel, crabs, skate and herring,
While others plot dire misdoings.

Oh what mischief
There is in a name,
A double wrongful slander
For the sake of alliteration;
Doing nature wrong my dear,
For them Seaford shags be cormorants,
No black-devil or harbingers
Of pestilence be they.
No my word.
Nor scavenging wreckers
Of poor souls
Lured by false hopes of safe haven.
Oh no my dear,
They be heraldic rock-throned sculptures,
Or sea-skimming, wave-diving
Submarine dancers;
That's what they be.
It's only us humans
That wave false harbour lights
On a steep shelved shore,
Promising salvation
But delivering tragedy.

Oh my, such wickedness.

Three grass hollows remain,
With sea-beet and skate boards,
Buttercups and ball games,
Daisies and dog walkers,
Kites and coffee-cups.
But nature's memory, long and fast,
Sends gulls to sit on phantom masts
Awaiting tides that made the past;
Through changing moons the waiting lasts.

Ghost Music

The Martello's relict cannon
Stands impotent guard
Over cappuccinos, choc-ices,
Pastel beach huts,
And on this sun-shone afternoon
Repels melancholy.

So we pluck optimism
Out of a calm sea,
Sky merging
Nearer than the horizon
But further than
The scale-sparkling,

Where an alchemy of sun-mist
Silvers scavenging crows,
Reforms unruly gulls
And drifts fishing boats
On impossible wings
Across elemental boundaries.

In and out
Of this soft-edged hemisphere,
Birds fly east and north
Towards fulfilment,
Lattice-patterning
With those at journey's end.

When ghost music sings
In spaces left by yesterday,
Mundane is somewhere else,
Uncertainty less urgent,
Loneliness less obvious
And infirmity less final.

The Hottest Day

The fleet is resting;
Thirteen boats beached,
Upended out of reach
Of high tides,

Chained to makeshift anchors
Securing their detention
From unwanted attention
Of gales and thieves.

Winches drag another
Clear of surf and foam
Across the subtle beauty of stones
And desiccated bladderwrack;

Then a long haul
Up a balconied beach
That contours the sweep
Of a wide curving bay,

Patterned by pastel patchworks,
Redolent with charcoal and lotions
That claim ownership
Of small patches of summer.

On this transitory boundary
Borrowed from the ocean
The elements are notionally benign;
When the tide is low

Groups cluster in confidence,
Wallowing in the clattering drag
With nagging concerns
For deeper dangers.

Others prefer the shore,
Testing skill and faith
As they spin cryptic spaces
For fantasy fish.

Beyond the baking beach
Kittiwakes gape and waul
Their eponymous calls
From sun-dazed cliffs;

And farther still,
Where a sea-mist lies,
Here and there are tied
Into one untroubled moment.

Doom Crows

Before the dawn can soften night
Remnant shards take furtive flight
From deep within the copse's shade;
They scatter as the Fates request
To seek out where misfortune rests
And scavenge where the spirit fades,
Where windows to the soul are misted
And frameworks of the body twisted.

Redeemers come in strange disguises,
Souls purged with strange devices
And dark preoccupations suppressed.
An old man walks the harbour's hollow,
Fifty demons in silence follow,
An entourage of obsequiousness.
He waves his hand, they flock to feed,
Their souls cleansed by scattered seed.

Sea-watching

Not good for May,
A strong north-easterly
With a grey chillness
That makes early morning
Unusually unattractive.

The promenade is bleak,
The wind eye-watering,
But a luminous sea
Defines the rim, clarifying
Space below deliquescent clouds.

Arriving from beyond the edge
Gannets in undulating lines
Convert benign brightness
Into lethal tines
Speared through wrinkled waves.

Gale-wise kittiwakes
Disregard mediocre squalls,
But not the hawkish skuas
That bully these gentle gulls
In intertwining ballets.

Between the milling wings
And hubbub of elements
Terns steer their fragility
Towards a greater wildness
And a beckoning destiny.

Before the month ends
All will be gone,
Taking alien excitement
Across myriad horizons
Towards a midnight sun.

Until then this concrete coast
Is transformed
By the visceral animation
Of the season's reforms
And an elation of purpose.

SEAFORD HEAD

Splash Point and Seaford Head 1860

At the eastern end of the promenade are the dramatic cliffs of Splash Point and Hawk's Brow, the most westerly part of Seaford Head. Somewhere on the slopes there was an abandoned chapel, probably very small, that was used as a hermitage by a recluse called Peter; he received royal protection in 1272, possibly for providing some service, such as a lookout. A legend of unknown vintage relates to Puck, a mischievous sprite, who had a 'church' situated on three almost inaccessible ledges at the end of a cleft in the cliffs.

Ledges on the cliffs, although limited and subject to frequent rock falls, are a home to a nesting colony of kittiwakes. These small gulls when not breeding, spend their time out at sea and although they were frequently seen around the Sussex coast, the first recorded breeding was in 1976 when four pairs nested at Newhaven. In the following years, a large colony built up between Newhaven and Peacehaven, with the first recorded nesting at Splash Point in 1989 when 46 pairs were counted.

This colony has continued to grow but has suffered, and will continue to suffer from periods of expansion and decline depending on the availability of food and nesting ledges.

Another coloniser is the fulmar petrel. These gull-like birds, small relatives of albatrosses, were only winter vagrants prior to 1945. By the 1950s they were regularly seen around the cliffs, prospecting the ledges and crevasses for nesting sites; although their numbers steadily increased, it was not until 1976 that breeding was confirmed.

Peregrine chicks taken from Seaford Head 1881

Peregrine falcons and ravens were a familiar part of the wildlife of the Sussex cliffs but both suffered from persecution and disappeared as breeding species; ravens were the first to go by about 1895 with peregrines hanging on until the 1950s, in spite of nest robbing by egg collectors, falconers and persecution during the Second World War. The Armed Forces were provided with 200,000 homing pigeons in the hope that airmen who had bailed out over enemy territory could attach details of their location to the birds and release them. Pigeons are a peregrine's favourite prey, so orders were given in 1940 to destroy these falcons, particularly along the south coast; even so, post-war a few pairs remained. However, the impact of agricultural pesticides on the viability of their eggs was the final straw and the last recorded breeding pair in Sussex nested on Seaford Head in 1956. When restrictions on some agricultural pesticides were introduced during the 1960s, peregrine numbers began and continue to increase, and both ravens and peregrines grace the Sussex cliffs again.

Splash Point has become one of the premier 'sea- watching' points along the Sussex coast where committed birdwatchers identify and record the numbers and species of birds flying up the Channel in the spring. While birds move up and down the coast throughout the year, this mass movement extends from early March to the end of May as migrating birds head north to their breeding areas. It can be very impressive if the wind is coming from the south-east when geese, ducks, wading birds, terns, gannets and small numbers of skuas are recorded. For most people though, this annual wildlife miracle of migration passes by unnoticed.

Seaford Head is designated as a nature reserve and managed with great beneficial effect for wild flowers and butterflies. Butterflies include such grassland specialities as dark-green fritillaries, Adonis blues and marbled whites; the rare silver-spotted skipper has also been recorded. Two migrant species, painted ladies and clouded yellows also make landfall on the Head during their journeys from the continent, with the former species being the most regular and abundant.

In spring the short turf is dotted with dog-violets and much smaller numbers of early purple and pyramidal orchids; in autumn, clustered bellflower, autumn gentian and the unassuming autumn ladies' tresses orchid provide interest. However, it is the summer plants such as birds-foot trefoil, sea pink, ladies bedstraw, bugloss, eyebright, centaury, knapweed and thyme that give uncultivated downland its magical colour and distinctive scent on long, warm days.

Not all the plants are benign. On the cliff edges, particularly where disturbed by rabbits, there are small colonies of henbane - the source of the narcotic, hyoscine. In the past this was used for treating a wide range of illnesses as well as a fanciful love potion. But if not treated with great care it can be lethal; it is claimed that Dr Crippen, the infamous Victorian, used it to kill his wife.

The nature reserve includes Hope Gap where the foreshore and near coastal area are of considerable importance for marine wildlife. Low tide exposes rock pools in a chalk platform that hold a range of marine animals including dog whelks, periwinkles, sea anemones, plus various crustaceans and fish such as gobies and blennies. As well as the sea-smoothed pebbles and chalk rocks on the beach, brown nodules of iron pyrites occur, which when split open reveal a shiny silvery-gold interior, commonly called fool's gold. Less frequently found are fossils of marine animals such as sea urchins. Due to their shape and patterns, these have been given a variety of common names such as shepherds' crowns, fairy loaves and thunderstones; they have been collected by people for thousands of years and at times attained a high degree of spiritual or magical significance.

The approaches to Hope Gap and the beach provide spectacular views of the Seven Sisters. These chalk cliffs originated some 300 million years ago when the land was covered by water and the shells of dead microscopic sea-life accumulated in a thick layer on the seabed. Over the millennia, this consolidated to form the soft rock that was later folded and moulded to form the South Downs. The flints that occur in dark strata in the chalk are a form of crystalline silica, hence their hardness and sharpness when split; these also were created from the skeletons of long–dead marine creatures.

The headlands of Beachy Head and Seaford Head provide habitats for breeding birds including stonechats, whitethroats and other scrub-loving birds, but they are best known as arrival and leaving points for a wide variety of migrant birds. This is most evident in autumn when large numbers of swallows and house martins congregate before heading off across the channel, often attracting the attention of hobbies, small migratory falcons, which specialise in feeding on fast-flying prey. Other autumn migrants occur on open ground. Small groups of yellow wagtails can be found feeding around the feet of sheep or cattle, but far more obvious are meadow pipits and wheatears, the latter being especially fond of newly ploughed fields. At the same time the remains of downland plants can be alive with birds such as linnets and goldfinches that feed on the abundant seeds; these flocks attract the attention of birds of prey including local sparrowhawks and the occasional migrant merlin.

On the steeper slopes of the dry valley called Hope Bottom, shrubs and small trees such as elder, blackthorn, privet and hawthorn flourish together with brambles, honeysuckle and wild clematis. As well as producing wonderful blossom, the fruits provide autumn food for migrating birds as they linger and build up their strength in preparation for their long journeys south. Species include a wide variety of warblers such as willow warblers, chiffchaffs, blackcaps, common whitethroats, lesser whitethroats and garden warblers. Nightingales, redstarts, spotted flycatchers and whinchats also occur in small numbers along with such scarce birds as wrynecks, firecrests and the occasional off-course rarity. As the autumn progresses starlings, redwings, song thrushes, fieldfares and large flocks of wood pigeons arrive from mainland Europe before moving inland to spend the winter months in Britain.

SEAFORD HEAD

THE POEMS

Puck Church

Splash Point

Not quite white,
Not quite perpendicular,
With temporary ledges
That blight would be
Adventurers

Is where a wildness begins;
For here the wind
Orchestrates misrule
Punishing the sins
Of the foolhardy.

Chaotic, spume sprayed,
Seaweed-slippy,
Sea-sculpted stones
Bar the way
To invaders

And a schizophrenic sea,
Gentle opalescence
Or mad-dog foamed,
Confirms the anarchy
Of the elements.

But the lightest of light
Disregard aeolian disorder,
Patterning the turbulence
In flight that contradicts
Commonsense.

Sanctuary calls
From tenement ledges
Urging delicate,
Dark-eyed gulls
To congregate on uncertainty;

Unsung seasonal symbols
Appearing from the
Nowhere of the ocean,
Singing from hymnals
Written in the configuration of stars.

Sea Pinks

No healing balm
Or fragrance to calm
The troubled surf of the mind;
Just clustered cushions, suffusing
The cliffs with blushing,
Where paint-bright gulls
Strut with reflected glory.

In this pastel flaunting
A wing-shadow haunting
By a lineage of appreciation;
Those buried close to the Gods,
Voyage-weary soldiers who trod
The chalk pathways
Hard by the airy drop;

The Saxon girl,
Winding pink chains to furl
Into her long hair,
Enriching loveliness
And subduing any sadness.
Later, Peter the Hermit
In his secluded cell,

Did he see God's power
In spring's bright flowers?
Or was it too seductive,
Too profane?
Too much the domain
Of Puck in his cliff-ledge parlour,
Sharing the wind with ravens,

Piping a mournful tune
While a gold-dust moon
Seduced the white Sisters,
Or dancing on the dew-cool turf
High above the pale strand's curve,
While Venus
Seared holes in the heavens.

The Apothecary's Garden

A dusting of unspecific sweetness drifts
A sun-released concoction,
Conjured from an apothecary's garden
Of sympathetic magic.

Ladies' tresses, mallow, gentian,
None too small to deserve attention;
Yellow bedstraw, trefoil, eyebright,
Garnered under sharp-shadowed moonlight;

Which, signified by God's benevolence,
Contain a physic trove
That brightens the eyes, cleans wounds
And challenges the poison of vipers.

Vervain, bugloss, bellflower, thyme,
Sweet as honey, strong as wine;
Mixed with dew for healing lotions,
Witches brew or heavenly potions?

Balanced on the fragile threshold
Between heaven and hell, they
Yield holy salves that ward off daemons
And all works of the devil.

Flowers of St John and centaury,
Knapweed, thistle, agrimony;
Rain-refreshed and sun-refined
Soothing souls and healing minds.

The Poisoner's Gift

Among the wind-waves
Lambs bleat unnecessary anguish,
And in the burning brightness
Seek painful comfort
From close-sheared ewes;

Maybe an uneasy inkling
Of the tenuousness of things;
Although the distant cliffs
Remain above the curdled edge
Of yet another falling tide

And skylarks renew
Their celebratory ascensions.
Below these disembodied melodies
An earthly pathway
Winds through a summary of life.

Here is the honey fragrance
Of a summer bed,
There, herbs of contentment
And the marbled fluttering
Of half-believed dreams;

And on the edge of oblivion
The interweaving threads
Of pain, lust and distress
Within the purple veins
Of a poisoner's gift.

Lost in Transit

Suggestions of tomorrow
Tint cloud-pallet skies,
Flecked with flickering
Signs of why

The time has come to leave
For summer birds;
Which, in their frantic silence
And urge to follow,

Ignore sad shades
Of the wasted lightness
Of journeys started
But never made;

Halted by snares
Of poverty on the Downs
And selfish gluttony
Of alien towns.

But the sweetness of ripening
And a bleeding of berries
Are recompense for ghosts
Of wind-blown feathers.

Venus and a New Moon

The sky is purged by ice
And urged by a shriving wind
To reveal its soul
Of healing brightness;
A reassuring lightness
Fixed above the dusty colours
Of the day's end.

When a silver paring
In celestial sharing
Creates a shocking beauty,
The moment loses meaning,
With forever seeming
Clear above the fast-fading
Outline of today.

Opening the door
Lets the magic restore
The fragile spirit,
Freeing the scars
That ache in the dark
Corners of yesterday
To scatter among the stars.

Easter Sonnet

Impatient for the blanching of blackthorn bushes
But soothed by vespers of prayerful thrushes;
Expecting soon the scimitar flighting
Across the dawn-downs' earlier brightening,
Urging the wind to cease its chafing
And end the violet's premature fading.
Inspired by the season's bold elation
No place for fear or contemplation,
No time for regret or to dwell on sorrow
Too soon today becomes tomorrow.

Spring Pictures

The solstice is past
And Lazarus elders revive
Their lichened limbs,
While crook-back blackthorn,
Star-pricked white,
Hints at a flowering
If the brisk northerly relents.

Romantic travellers are stalled
But the sedentary progress;
Ignoring the tardiness
Of iconic prodigals
Before-dawn blackbirds
And dusk-veiled thrushes
Maintain the momentum.

High above the gorse's
Dust of powdered gold
A peregrine's ominous arc
Hangs below the benign paleness
Of a mid-day moon,
While jackdaws voice
Querulous consternation.

Beyond the hedge, numbered lambs
Bleatingly seek matching mothers;
In the distance, torn veils drag shadows
Across a purpling forest
And subterfuge brightness
Illuminates the mixed emotions
Of a confused landscape.

Hope Beach

The wind's mixed blessing
Sullies the sea's palette,
Polishes the sky
And falsifies the colour of wings
That ghost-shade the purified cliffs,
Mocking our tethering shadows.

So sift the chaos of pebbles,
The swirls, whorls,
Cones and slippers of whelks,
Cockles and limpets
To discover the magic
Of a shepherd's crown.

Take uneasy steps
On the jagged pavement
Pitted by the passage
Of seahorse hooves,
Riddled by the rasping
Of phantom tongues

And follow pied-pipers
To the sanctuary of imagination.
Listen to seductive hushing
From mermaid rocks
Where seven whistlers seven times
Trill omens of apocalypse;

Then, throwing doubt
Into the enchanted well
Lined by mad-mind sculpting
And myth-green hair
Of rock-pool sprites,
Unfurl your wings.

CUCKMERE VILLAGES

Alfriston Village Centre

The farming and fishing communities that lived in the Cuckmere valley no doubt created landing stages on the inlets and creeks that extended through the intertidal saltmarsh. It is likely that in Saxon times Exceat, Westdean and Chyngton had small harbours; Alfred the Great had a palace at Westdean and it is possible that Exceat was an important Anglo-Saxon naval base. In medieval times the salt marsh and mud flats would have also been utilised for salt production, important and valuable for seasoning and preserving food. This process declined and disappeared with the silting up of the estuary and the drainage of salt marsh for the summer grazing of livestock.

The Doomsday Book of 1086 details the number of heads of households of the Cuckmere valley communities; Westdean had 70, Exceat 50, Wilmington 100, Charleston 45 and

Alfriston just 30. However, in the 14th and 15th centuries, poor harvests, the impact of the Black Death and French raids saw the breakdown of whole communities - some never recovered. Exceat was one such community and by the early 15th century it had disappeared for ever except for the remains of its church.

When conditions improved in the 16th century, populations increased. However, this did little to rejuvenate most of the Cuckmere villages as the enclosure of common land had destroyed a rural way of living and the population had drifted away, firstly into the Weald as it became available for agriculture and industry and later into the industrialising towns. Even when sheep farming on the Downs became more lucrative in the late 18th century, it did little to improve the availability of jobs for the rural workforce as one shepherd and his dogs could 'manage' large areas of land for most of the year.

When arable farming began to flourish in the 19th and 20th centuries the ever-increasing mechanisation of farming prevented any revival of rural communities; even if the villages endured, most became 'villages' in name only, being more a collection of houses than fully functioning entities with shops, trades and schools. However, where churches survived into the 19th century they have been restored, are cared for and hold periodic services.

Alfriston appears to be very different – the ancient, large and very beautiful church, the shops, restaurants, inns and hotels together create an atmosphere of timeless prosperity; but this is an illusion. Even by the year 1360 when the church was built exactly as it is today, there were probably only 100 or so people living in the village; just why the church is so large and impressive is unknown. It is likely that there was a smaller Saxon church on the site and it is also suggested that the mound on which the church stands was raised in pre-Christian times as a site for pagan worship.

However, Alfriston has a number of attributes that have served it well and enabled it to survive the periodic social and economic downturns that so damaged other villages. It is situated on the banks of a small but navigable river that gives direct access to the sea, it is close to a long-established river crossing at Winton Street and its position below the northern edge of the Downs makes it close to transport links to the east or west and to settlements in the Weald. Thus, over time, it became a centre for the local agricultural community, providing regular markets and annual stock fairs and facilities for food and accommodation for traders and travellers. The farmers also required the services of blacksmiths, millers, farriers and basket makers, and the products and by-products of farming provided the raw materials for small local commercial enterprises such as tanning, shoemaking and glove-making. All these farmers, tradespeople and their families required the services of butchers, bakers, drapers, hat-makers, innkeepers and grocers, and village life flourished.

Although Alfriston was not a 'port', the river Cuckmere provided a limited but important commercial link to and from the world outside the valley. In the 18th century, imported cargoes included beach shingle and chalk for road building, domestic fuel, timber, seaweed for agricultural fertilizer, oil cake for cattle and retail stores; the cargoes for return journeys included products of the tanning industry and wool from downland sheep. In the early 19th century two barges, the Adventurer and the Good Wife traded between Alfriston and Newhaven.

Thus the village had an inbuilt self-sufficiency that enabled the growth of a comfortable and increasingly wealthy group of tenant farmers, tradespeople and skilled artisans who owned land and property in and around the area. Even the Napoleonic Wars that began in 1793 were beneficial as the troops billeted in and around Alfriston provided a large and captive market for the village's goods and services. But this picture is incomplete, for under this prosperity were landless labourers who worked on farms, on the roads and in local industries; they bore the brunt of any social and economic downturns yet were in no position to benefit from any subsequent upturns in fortunes. They lived in highly overcrowded, damp, dark, insanitary and cold cottages and for some, the harsh conditions of the workhouse were preferable.

But it was not just the labouring poor who were vulnerable to change. The end of the Napoleonic Wars in 1815 heralded a decline of prosperous local industries as markets for their goods suddenly disappeared. Later, access to and from the Cuckmere valley was improved by the advent of rail transport; a line was opened in 1846 that passed through the nearby village of Berwick linking the area to Hastings in the east, to Lewes and Brighton in the west and thence to all stations to London. This gave local people access to markets outside the village and, over time, the self-sustaining economy began to collapse. People again drifted into the towns to seek work and the village slipped into a rapid spiral of decline. In the early years of the 1900s the parish church's finances were frequently in deficit and in 1915 the last barge, the Iona, made its final journey.

The mid-eighteenth century development of the villages of Eastbourne and Brighton as seaside resorts did little for the Cuckmere villages. These communities were isolated by rutted and dusty or muddy farm tracks and lacked any of the facilities and attractions required by the health and pleasure-seeking metropolitan wealthy. But this isolation suited George, Prince of Wales; in 1784 he met, fell in love with and later secretly married Maria Fitzherbert. To carry out this clandestine relationship they rented Clapham House in the small village of Litlington under the names of Mr and Mrs Payne and two of their children were born there. Maria Fitzherbert was a Catholic and as no member of the British Royal Family was allowed by law to marry a Catholic, the marriage was not recognised and George was forced to marry his cousin, Princess Charlotte, in 1795.

One of the gardeners at Clapham House was John Russell, who when times were hard in the early 1800s, rented land in Litlington and started a fruit-growing business. When he died in 1862 his sons took over and developed the commercial orchards into ornamental gardens, decorative orchards and facilities for catering. These were re-branded as Pleasure Gardens and opened to the public. By this time the growth of the railways had made the coast accessible and seaside holidays had become immensely popular among the Victorian middle classes. The Times newspaper of 1841 commented: 'Among those who are well-to-do the annual trip to the seaside has become a necessity of which their fathers never dreamt'. The Pleasure Gardens matured and became very popular, with visitors transported from hotels in Eastbourne and from the train station at Berwick to enjoy a day out at Litlington. By the late 1860s parties of up to 130 people were enjoying elaborate meals, sports, river swimming and fishing. The Gardens, now renamed as 'Tea Gardens', are still providing refreshments for today's tourists to the valley.

After the First World War car ownership increased and the open landscapes and quaint villages of the South Downs soon became a favourite destination for wealthy 'weekenders' and escapees from London. When the bicycle became a popular and affordable means of transport, Sussex became accessible to many more tourists eager to take advantage of the network of lanes, footpaths and bridleways that criss-cross the Downs. Visits to Sussex were no doubt encouraged by the enormous amount of poetry and prose written by Victorian and Edwardian writers who were fulsome in their praise of the rural charms of Sussex. To add to the Litlington gardens, other facilities were developed at Berwick in 1925 and at Exceat in the 1930s. Today this trend continues, with the beauty and accessibility of the landscapes and the picturesque charm of the villages contributing to the large tourist economy of the area.

CUCKMERE VILLAGES

THE POEMS

Lullington Church

Cuckmere Hauntings

The cogs are winding down
And the year in no-when time,
Colours are shades of weary
As the year subsides
Into becalming melancholy.

But the tipping point beckons;
Swallows are uneasy,
Warblers caution from elder glades
And ochreous Downs
Cast an earlier shade.

Mornings rise from mist,
Nights have chilling edges
And ghost-winged owls
Fan rosehip sparks
In autumn-kindled hedges.

Other hauntings tell stories
Of tending stock, of tilling earth,
Of gleaning a hedgerow wage,
Of lives that came then quickly spent
On the valley's indifferent stage.

Poynings' Town

It has been a year that favours
Lambing, the best
The farmer can remember.
Dazzle-bright days to savour,
Warm where the wind can't reach,
The nights with no frost
To speak of, and the fields
Sun-dried and winter bleached.

Already the first-born
Are on the hill.
Those that came later
Behind castles of corn,
And pampered by aromatic hay
Practice their
Spring-time responsibility
Of unsteady play.

But come tomorrow,
Ewes in the far barn
Will journey into familiar fields;
Their lambs will follow
Into the glare of early spring,
With a mother's fleece
Between them and whatever
The remnant winter brings.

On the concave brow,
Wind-moulded sycamores
Make elliptical darkness
Of substance and shadow;
In this sculpted grove
Rooks in fretful conversations
Build high or low
As the wind behoves.

When birds sing Arcadia to sleep,
Phantoms of what might have been
Flicker around the hillside
And creep into the dusk;
Hammer on nails, the crack
Of adze on stone,
Until rippling flames
Burn the silence back.

No phoenix is reborn;
From under the broken walls
A trotting fox, a shuffling badger
Cause the ewes to turn,
With lambs pressed
Close to watch them pass.
Night advances
And the hill is repossessed.

A Day by the Sea 1920

We will take a boat my darling man
Unhitch it from the river's side,
Then drift to where the sparkling flow
Meets with a wave-flecked tide.
We will moor the boat to a weed-hung post
And scramble to the shore;
We will lay the picnic blanket down
And sleep in dreamless peace once more.

Why hide your face my bravest man
When the day is brightly shining?
It's the stone-grey faces in the tide
Whose dead eyes scorn my living.
Oh no my dear, it's just the weeds
That in the current waft and wallow
And the shadows of the fish that rise
To feed among the shallows.

Why cling so tight my fearful man
When there's laughter in the air?
It's the bodies scattered on the beach
In broken poses lying there.
Oh no, it's just the couples dear
Who lie among the sea-shore flowers,
Spreading limbs to the warming sun
And sharing longed-for hours.

What pains you so my tear-wracked man
When our love is strong and deep?
It's the mud-caked mouths that gape and wail
And pray for endless sleep.
Oh no my dear, it's just the gulls
That search the jetsam rime,
Their lost-soul-crying mournfulness
Carries on the wind.

Why close your ears my hiding man
When larks sing high and sweet?
It's the clattering gunfire beyond the brow
Destroying all it meets.
Oh no my dear, please listen hard
Above your fears and hurt,
It's just the stones when waves retreat
That rattle in the surf.

Why toss and turn my restless man
When the blanket's soft and warm?
It's the mud that clings and sucks you down
To those who died all twisted torn.
Oh no my dear, it's just the sand
Where small birds pipe and feed,
It drains into the current's flow
And sighs as the tide recedes.

Golden Ages

Lingering by the umber gleam
Of a lethargic river
Or surveying soft-sculpted hills,
Dreamers dream
Of a golden age
Where ruddy yeomen
And sturdy boatmen
Work tides and seasons.

Marvelling at facades
Of renovated antiquity,
Wishful thinkers conjure
Colourful promenades
Around the market cross,
While romantic rogues,
Warmed by open fires,
Plot illegal trade.

Drink wine
Where the village quenched
Its thirst, eat fine cake
Where the village
Baked its bread,
Kneel and pray
Where the village prayed
And complete the idyll;

At best a deception
Of simplification, at worst
An intolerance of blemishes
Which spoil the perception
Of a village of confident sufficiency
At one with itself,
With God
And with Nature.

But from the damp shade,
There by the Poor House wall
Or under the hedgerow's edge,
A miasmic chant swells and fades:
Remember us;
My children die, my wife is sick,
My spirit broken;
Remember us.

Garden Party

Quick, quick the sun might fade
So paint the canvas bright
And touch light in the eyes
With strokes of happiness.
Then, before the movement starts,
Arrange silent conversations
In clustered creations
Caught in filigreed shade.

Quick, quick before the colour leaves
Fleck the background through
With wing-flickered blue
Of lavender and buddleia.
Then, before the apples fall,
Put laughter on the faces
And music in the spaces
Between drought-tired trees.

Quick, quick before the warmth has gone
Hold the season still,
Don't let the garden fill
With tomorrow.
Quick before the picture dries
Put dancing feet
In the gilding heat
Then let the autumn come.

Corelli on the Tye

The day suspending
Somewhere between the seasons,
In a never land
Of wishful thinking
Where the poplars' desiccated quivering
Sifts memories between now
And a beginning.

Swallows' and picnics' gentle deluding
Trick the day-dreaming year
Into fantasies
Of things everlasting,
Until gulls' angelic ghosting
Turns the mind to
Thoughts of inevitable losing.

Then music's intervening
Sings yesterday into
The consciousness of today;
Confirming time's passing
A violin's hurtful soaring
Bites acid-deep
Until tears quench the burning.

When a cello's insistent sobbing
Repeats the message,
One cry leads to another
To drown the throbbing
Of this new tune's keening,
Until another leaves the minor key
To relieve the mourning.

The Smallest Church

Hidden
From casual passers-by
Who may not register why
Such remnants are significant,
And from prying eyes
That may see only
Quaint curiosity.

Discrete fingers
Point the way
And narrow paths
Linger by a garden
Of controlled neglect;
Careless delight
In a careful mingling

Of overblown roses,
Marguerites, cranesbill,
Poppies and rosemary.
Ash and elms border
A view to the hills
From the place
A seat would fill

Under an orchard of eleven trees.
A poor harvest to come,
Perhaps a glut last year
That filled cupboards with
Jam and chutney
And wine brewed
From elder and blackberry.

Though barely past spring,
An antique gate
Reveals high-summer torpor;

A sedation of flies drones
Around sun-warmed stones
And a thrush intones
Day-dream chanting.

Sun-beamed through
A palisade of trees,
A sanctuary of calm
Protected from harm
By a ridge of Downs
And moats of manicured wheat
Half-seen through discrete frames.

A hesitant kestrel
Checks in enchantment
Above the chancel, clean painted
And newly shingled.
Perhaps an elegant
Ivied and lichened ruin
Would be a more poignant

Accompaniment to the
Overgrown stones
Of previous dimensions,
Not large, but enough
For an unknown village;
Perhaps skeletons, ghosts
And wind-soft moaning

More fitting memorials
To the burning and decay
Of church and community.
But a valiant bell
Calls the faithful to pray
And murmur hymns
To the harmonium's harmony.

'The Lord hath given
And the Lord hath taken away,
Praise be the Lord
For the sacrifice of yesterday.'
Today, columbine drops
Venous purple across the reredos
Of myth and mystery;

A pelican feeds its young
With the blood of its breast,
The chalice, the crucifix,
The sacrificial lamb is blessed.
Oh the hell of getting to heaven
Set amongst the heaven
Of the earth at rest.

Sundial at Litlington Church

Stark shadows of summer
Mark lingering days,
Winter sun hurries
Fitful hours into
Early oblivion,
Bright moons
Move silvered moments
And pale lamplight fixes
Time on the wall.

But wind and rain
Have rusted and eroded
And time has ended;
As once it ended
For three children
From the Rectory.
'For these things I weep,
My eyes dissolve,
For a comforter is far from me,
One to revive my courage.'

Above the gate
The flag of St George
Is wind-battle torn,
The millennium lamp rusted;
Moon daisies, valerian
And toadflax overgrow
Gnarled flint walls;
Bedstraw, mullein
And speedwell reclaim
The graveyard.

Inside, time is on hold.
For the moment
Bell ropes hang limp;

By the organ old red shoes
Wait for dancing feet;
At the pulpit, faded lilies,
On the altar, roses,
Delphiniums and carnations
Droop and drop
Their papered petals.

So go back,
Place a twig in the centre
Of the dial to
Restart the clock.
The bells will ring,
The organ sound,
Children will play
In the meadow
And withered flowers revive.

Fireside Thoughts

At the end of a difficult day,
A communion to administer
And a burial a horse ride away,
I do enjoy the mellow warmth
Of a good brandy and a pipe
Of fine tobacco by the hearth.

Of course I abhor
Those whose lives include
Breaking the law.
But does not the Good Lord feed
And support the weak
In their times of need?

My flock deserves bread and ale
When crops, fishing
Or employment fail;
It is my calling's decreeing
That I care for both earthly
And spiritual well-being.

It is the King's pocket the customs line
And he will not miss payments
On a few barrels of wine,
Or brandy or tea or lace
Which looks so fine
Below my good wife's face.

But violence I reject,
The beatings and burnings
Are acts to which I strongly object.
The perpetrators are not my congregation;
It is that Godless gang upstream
That brings such defamation

To enterprising free trade.

Maybe I should withdraw?
But I have been dismayed
After a night of frequent alarms
To find my horse hard-worked,
A cargo hidden in my barn

And a barrel left as recompense;
Which of course I cannot return,
As it makes no sense
To put my flock in jeopardy
With the law.
It would be foolhardy,

For what good to child or wife
Is an imprisoned husband
And his ruined life?
So for the greater good
I turn a blind eye
As any compassionate man would.

Westdean

They knew that natural
Gargoyles grew, layered
In an architecture of chalk;
A blessing for builders,
A curse for ploughmen
And the cottager's fork.

They carted them here,
Planted them layer on layer,
And the village grew from toil
On the sea, salt-marsh,
Fragrant turf
And pale brown soil.

Fickle tides change
And history's lottery rearranges
Fortunes and futures.
Now no voices in the wind,
No clatter in the streets;
Only flints endure.

Names identify
Reworked remains of what
Flourished in seclusion.
The barns and forge
Were, but are not,
And the Manor an illusion.

The Church stays open,
Services on alternate Sundays
And weekday worship survives;
But with noble memorials
And sculpted heads
No tributes to humble lives.

Even the forest has no ghosts
Among the regiment host
Of invading trees;
Ivy is a gesture of disorder,
Primroses and violets
A tenacious continuity.

Beyond the valley's fold
Uncompromising wheat holds
No songs or singers.
But on the hard trodden track
And by the wayfarer tree
Shadows linger.

The Last Oxen

There should be a monument here,
Standing bold on the brow,
Bronze to show strength
With nobility in wide-spread horns.
Lamb and Leader mark the goad,
Pilot, Pedlar, haul the load,
Quick and Nimble, Ay and Gee
Walk us into history.

For this is where a story ends,
It began somewhere else
And why it ended, like most stories,
Was merely a matter of time.
Place a cowslip in my coat,
Tie a kerchief at my throat;
Steer the plough and guide the harrow,
Prepare the earth for wheat tomorrow.

The design must honour a life of service,
Tramping fields, yoked and muzzled,
To feed Britons, Saxons, Normans
And on until that unmarked day.
Hard-up my lovelies,
We'll plough from seven till three,
Then stand-hard kids if the acre's done,
Remove the yokes, fate's web is spun.

The epitaph must evoke a sadness
Of lost connections to the land,
To the subtlety of seasons
And to belonging.
We'll trudge our way towards the farm
To stalls within the flint-built barn,
We'll feed you well on hay and straw,
Then rest yourselves until the dawn.

Exceat

Imagination runs like a fox
In a witch-making wind;
Skipping and spinning while
Black-tipped ears turn to find
The sculpted elder's scratch and scree,
Telling stories of what might be
Hidden in the substance of turf and tree
And the gargoyle nuggets of flint.

To find these not-even memories
I take the accustomed way that etches
A track to where a sweep of
Soft-curve slopes stretches
Around a contained compass.
Here the church stood, and I look east
Towards the horseshoe apse
Where the altar focussed lives.

I see sheep folded on the fallow,
Dark oxen leading the plough,
And smoke above the steep-pitch thatch.
I could give thanks with you now
Or wait until St Hilary's night is past,
Or until a Pascal moon rises
Over Haven Brow sending silver shafts
Across blackthorn's spring snow.

From the west door
I see water meadows and salt marsh
Where boats seek sanctuary
Against the season's harsh infidelities.
I see gulls in luminous squalls,
The soft edge of clouds
Laced into the sea's grey thrall,
So I can warn of storms approaching.

To the south, two headlands frame
A cleft of sea and bound the haven,
So I can watch for ominous sails
And warn of craven intent.
From the porch on the north wall
I see travellers on the bostal
With sickness in their footfall,
So I will weep with you.

But there is music beyond the wind;
To the chants of Mass and David's psalms
I will kneel and pray with you;
With tabor, pipe and astringent shawms
I will join the line and dance with you;
To the soft-plucked harp I will sing
A lament for the home you knew
And the unkindness of fate.

THE CUCKMERE VALLEY

Cuckmere River at Alfriston

The Cuckmere is described as the only unspoiled and undeveloped river valley in Sussex. Unspoiled yes, but unaltered no, and if history had played out differently the valley could well have succumbed to housing or industrial developments.

By 1347, Seaford and its surrounding land was the property of the Poynings family and it is reputed that sometime around 1350, due to Seaford's dilapidated state, Michael, Lord Poynings, obtained permission to build a new town on the Downs on the west side of the lower Cuckmere valley – Poynings' Town. Little else is known, although excavations in the mid 1800s found considerable evidence of foundations and debris of buildings in the area named on maps as Walls Brow. Some of the debris showed signs of burning, suggesting that even before the town could be completed it was destroyed by fire; if, how or why this happened is unrecorded.

Much later, in 1836, plans were put forward to build a hotel and a development of over 2,000 houses in an area of open downland to the north of Exceat bridge, and in the 1920s, a housing development at Crowlink on the Seven Sisters was a serious possibility. Both plans failed, the latter largely due to a public outcry that attracted the support of the national press and led to the creation of what is now called the South Downs Society. Proposals for other potentially very intrusive industrial and tourism developments came and went. In 1897 a plan was put forward for a nine-mile light railway system to link Birling Gap, West Dean, Litlington and Alfriston to the main line at Berwick. This did not materialize, but a narrow-gauge railway carried shingle, extracted from the beach at Cuckmere Haven, to a cleaning and storage depot at Exceat. The shingle was used for house and road building and operations were active from the 1930s until 1964. From the 1920s, there was a tea room close to the beach with vehicular access enabling the creation of an informal camping site and in 1936, a plan was proposed for the development of a 'pleasure beach' on the site. This did not come to fruition but a small caravan park was set up on the slopes of Cliff End and Haven Brow; when it was removed in the early 1970s the lower Cuckmere valley assumed its appearance of timeless serenity.

For many centuries the area's economy was based on wheat and sheep with catch-crops of turnips and legumes grown in rotation as fodder for livestock. The sheep were not only a source of wool and mutton, but also mobile organic fertilisers for the arable land. Ploughing, in the main, was carried out by teams of dark-red Sussex oxen, used in Britain as beasts of burden from as far back as 300 BC. Horses were not utilised until after the Norman Conquest and their use varied considerably from region to region for, although horses were quicker and more manoeuvrable, oxen were stronger and cheaper to feed and maintain. As Sussex suffered considerable rural poverty, oxen were used extensively throughout the 19th century and were still in use into the 20th century; the last working team in England was based at Exceat farm and was sold on October 15th 1925.

A viable sheep-based economy did not develop until the late 18th century when John Ellman of Glynde bred Southdown sheep which had both soft wool and high quality meat. This resulted in the spread of close-cropped, sheep covered downland watched over by shepherds and their dogs. Although shepherds were highly respected members of the agricultural community, their wages were low and they often augmented their income by catching two species of downland birds, wheatears and skylarks. Wheatears, which are little larger than a house sparrow, are summer visitors to Britain and were in particular demand by wealthy gourmets who visited the growing and increasingly fashionable towns of Brighton and Eastbourne. These small birds were sold for 18 pence a dozen and a shepherd could earn anything between £4 and £20 a year.

Wheatears nest in disused rabbit burrows and crevices or holes in walls which, due to the openness of downland, also provide security from aerial predators. Shepherds took advantage of this and placed horsehair nooses at the entrance of specially dug shallow pits to snare the birds. The season for wheatears opened on St James's day, July 25th and lasted until the end of September, a period coinciding with the increase in population at the completion of the local breeding season and the influx of more northerly breeding birds heading south for the winter.

Wheatears are still common in Sussex as spring and autumn migrants but unfortunately few now stay to breed, the majority of them on coastal sites. However, their demise has more to do with changes to farming methods than to the actions of downland shepherds.

Other people were also involved in bird-catching as there was a trade in wing and tail feathers for hat decoration and a market for live birds, goldfinches and linnets especially, for the cage-bird trade. Also, when families could not afford meat, large numbers of birds such as blackbirds and thrushes were trapped to be used as pie filling. Trapping of small birds slowly disappeared in the late 19th and early 20th century when the practice was censured and denounced as barbaric, and no doubt as rural populations decreased and extreme poverty began to decline.

The short grazed turf of open downland with its wide diversity of plants and animals cannot be described as a 'natural habitat' as it is the product of centuries of tree clearance and stock grazing. This ancient lineage means that it is considered to be the natural 'destiny' of the eastern South Downs. However, when the economic benefits of arable farming increased, large areas of the Downs were converted to arable crop growing, especially wheat. Sadly, the use of inorganic fertilizers and pesticides and the removal of copses and hedgerows to make way for mechanised, highly efficient ploughing and harvesting have created large swathes of ecologically diminished farmland. This can still look beautiful, but has resulted in dramatic declines in butterflies, wild flowers, and birds such as corn buntings, grey partridges, lapwings and skylarks.

Other changes to farming practices over the centuries and the increasing pressures of human disturbance have caused the disappearance of two charismatic downland breeding birds; stone curlews becoming extinct as a breeding species in the late 1980s and the great bustard over a hundred years earlier. This dramatic turkey-sized bird was prized as a food item and later, as it became rarer, egg and skin collectors added to the pressure. It became extinct in Sussex probably in the early 1820's, not long before it was lost to Britain as a whole.

Another species to suffer the same fate is the cirl bunting. They declined rapidly in the mid 1960s but remained a familiar bird in the lower Cuckmere valley; 12 to 15 pairs were recorded in the 1970s but the decline continued and they no longer breed in Sussex.

Fortunately, some farmers have changed their land management and cropping practices, greatly improving the ecological diversity of their farms while maintaining productive and profitable businesses. In these areas the decline of some species is being halted.

Friston Forest is something of an anomaly on the largely unwooded East Sussex Downs. However, it is a man-made forest of relatively recent origin, a process that began towards the end of the 19th century and continued throughout the first half of the 20th. Its functions were two-fold. Before the creation of the forest the land was acquired by the Eastbourne Waterworks Company which, by tapping into the aquifers, was able to secure a water supply for the rapidly growing coastal town. After the experiences of the 1st World War, the Forestry Commission leased the area to provide a home-grown source of general purpose timber that would safeguard supplies in the event of another conflict. Although this created a woodland habitat, the regimented and high density planting was of limited value for wildlife. However, with maturation and vast improvements in forest management, Friston Forest now provides habitats for an ever-increasing number of woodland plants and animals, including white helleborine orchids, white admirals and buzzards; the latter are rapidly re-colonising after years of persecution.

Over the years, the river Cuckmere has been extensively managed to improve navigation, to improve summer grazing and to protect the villages from flooding. No doubt regular maintenance took place at the time of the earliest settlements; however, the first reference to this, a widening of the river north of Exceat bridge, dates from the early 17th century. Plans for major work date from 1792 and culminated in 1847 when excavations to straighten the course of the river from Exceat south to Chyngton were carried out, thus creating the meanders or 'ox-bow' lakes; the last realignment took place in 1938 when the river was straightened to the north of Exceat.

River management has had a major impact on the ecology of the valley and there are virtually no intertidal mudflats or salt marshes. Thus many of the plants and animals that are a common feature of other river estuaries are absent or in short supply and although it is still a beautiful place, it is devoid of much of the music, colour and movement of larger estuaries. The lack of flocks of wading birds and wildfowl that are such an attractive feature of the West Sussex estuaries and harbours is particularly noticeable. If estuarine habitats were present, some of the thousands of birds that pass up and down the Channel at migration times would undoubtedly stop off in the valley to rest, feed and for some, find winter refuge. At the moment only small numbers of birds such as bar-tailed godwits, whimbrel, grey plover, ringed plover and dunlin occur, while occasionally, and spectacularly, ospreys pass through the valley in both spring and autumn. The winter months show little improvement with only small numbers of curlews, oystercatchers and redshank present and although wigeon numbers are reasonable, only small numbers of teal and shelduck and occasionally brent geese or white-fronted geese join the large groups of non-native Canada geese.

Extensive drainage of the water meadows has also depleted the numbers of breeding birds and species such as yellow wagtail, snipe and redshank nest rarely if at all. Fortunately the valley still boasts a small heronry, and the tree-nesting grey herons along with little egrets, their smaller, more delicate and bright white relatives, are easily seen in the ditches and ponds, along the river's edge or on the shoreline. Little egrets are very welcome newcomers to the valley; they were first recorded in Sussex in 1952 and even in the 1980s were very rare. In the 1990s numbers increased dramatically, particularly in West Sussex and in 1996 almost 100 birds were counted at a roost site in Chichester harbour. At this time they started to appear in the lower Cuckmere valley and are now seen all year round, with the largest numbers occurring in late summer and autumn.

The inevitable process of climate change is destined to impact on sea levels, weather patterns and coastal erosion. In the light of this, the Environment Agency decided in 2009 to cease funding the maintenance of the riverbanks of the lower Cuckmere valley. Instead it will focus its efforts and finances on flood defences in the more populated areas of the region, while making a commitment to keep the river mouth open until a self–managing estuary is re-established. Once this takes place the lower Cuckmere should become home to a far greater range of plants, mammals and birds. It will change in appearance, but it will develop a new and greater beauty, as the natural world takes over this very small fragment of a crowded coastline that, in the main, is dedicated to human habitation, enterprise and recreation.

THE CUCKMERE VALLEY

THE POEMS

The Seven Sisters, Hope Gap and Cuckmere Haven from Seaford Head

Seven Sisters

The cliffs' extravagant perspective
Slopes towards the sea mist;
Untroubled faces of chalk and flint
Of here today and here tomorrow,
Unworried brows of turf and thorn
Of here this spring and here the next.

Long before the image
Disappears into uncertainty,
A destination of comfortable distance,
And between here and there
A reliable beauty purified
Of the jetsam of tide and time.

But crossing the river towards
The unambiguous edge,
Mournful shawms of gulls,
A falcon's harsh alarms
And a raven's resonant foreboding
Challenge permanence.

For substance is chipped away
In a never-ending sculpting,
Rendering histories and futures
As cobwebs of sound,
The quick-silver of surf
Or fragments of rainbows.

But skylarks, yesterday forgotten,
Tomorrow unconceived,
Their tentative winter murmurings
Cast off, fill the space
Between now and nowhere
And celebrate the moment.

Folk Song

The sweep-sloped downs are greening,
The ewes and lambs content,
The larks sing high as summer
Though winter is scarcely spent.

There is an exaltation
Somewhere and nowhere,
Filling the hemisphere
Pitched above the wide horizon.
There is hopefulness
In the framework of winter,
Strengthening anticipation
With songs of tomorrow.

A chaffinch sings a serenade
From trees still bare-branch wan
And rooks are building higher,
So sure that winter is done.

There is healing
In the sun-musk fragrance,
Gold-dust bright
In the sharpness of memory.
There is a newness
In the winter-washed,
Wind-scoured whiteness
That separates green from grey.

The gorse is freed from burning
And chasing daemons done,
Its flowers now sweet with honey
Show winter is dead and gone.

There is exuberance
In the turbulent
Wind-draught soaring
That celebrates being;
There is a cleansing
In the fast-flow water
Taking histories
Beyond the torn-lace surf.

Remains of cold-sky raining
Are carried home at last,
The sparkled run and ripple
Deem winter's time is passed.

Colours of November

In a luminous dawn
Remnants of rainbows
Radiate from a rising sun,
And rainbow birds
Rapier across the rising
Tide's reckless river race.

In a monochrome morning
Curlews mark time until the
Malingering tide turns,
Their melancholy music
Murmuring from meadows
And meandering marshes.

On a dazzled afternoon
A refining sun gilds
The gleaning geese,
And where the gorse greets
A glistering sea,
Transforms the gliding gulls.

In a translucent evening
A winter owl wheels high
On a whirling wind,
While a winter moon
Rises full and white
Over a frosted wildness.

Cuckmere Illusions

Cloud strands conjure colours
From the rising sun;
A wave of the wind wand
Chases rose blooms
Across the moment
And slings apricot paths
Across infinity.

Drifting mist enchants the air
With promises;
A wave of the wind wand
Paints the buttressed cliffs
With gold dust
And sends a plated river
To sanctuary in the sea vaults.

Spiders' webs weave spells
On the prosaic;
A wave of the wind wand
Sends shooting stars
Across hawthorn shade
And sparkles jewel strings
Between desiccated stems.

Water pools bewitch eyes
With earth skies;
Another wave of the wind wand
Shatters the mirror,
Scattering illusions
And rendering magic
Mere tricks of the light.

The Cusp of the Seasons

Currents and tides
Slow-sculpted the
Valley's smooth-curve slopes,
Scoured the flood plain
And crafted a broad
Constancy.
At slack low tide
The river wallows
And mullet rise
In sun-warmed shallows.

Lichened fences,
Gates and stiles,
Smoothed and shone
By anonymous hands
Are reference points
In the season's helter-skelter.
This year, next year,
Will the links be severed?
Walk the banks
And hope for never.

Gulls chased by
Ghosts of transience
Slip-drift across the scarp
And swifts' shrill hysterics
Pierce as they leave the
Safety of the void.
Tethered by shadows'
Ripple glide
They wait for clouds
To loosen ties.

In the urgency
Of temporality,
Whitethroats tempt fate
In aerial excursions
And linnets suspend trinkets
From hawthorn twigs.
The simple songs
Of scratch and jingle
With spring's white lattice
Drift and mingle.

On the cusp
Of the seasons, a cavalcade
Of exuberant gold
On the meadows
And a synthesis of whiteness
On the breeze.

On the Edge of Things

It is a becalming time
As a flotsam of blackthorn,
Timber from forgotten wrecks
Tangle-tied in garish twine,
Drifts on fitful ripples;
Then with a scum of silt
Turns to jetsam that stipples
The reedy edge.

It is a waiting time
As green is silvered
By the willow's winnowing,
Whitened by elder's shine
And flushed by
Trellises of wild roses
That hesitate on the
Edge of summer's rush.

It is a reflecting time,
On opportunities missed
Or preparations complete.
In the crowfoot rime,
Balanced in the scaffold sedge
An abandoned nest,
And beyond, a song sung
On the edge of fulfilment.

It is an introspective time
As a fox's amber stare
Engages across the divide,
Consigning intruders
To another stage.
Dismissed, I take my place
On the edge
Of the season's turning page.

Of Magpies and Rainbows

I have the measure of magpies' contradictions;
One for sorrow, two for joy
And doff your cap to avoid afflictions.
But how many curlews does it take
To siren sadness into a cryptic marsh,
How many egrets to illuminate
The shadowland of depression?
How many gulls in spiralling flight
To draw anxiety into the vortex
And how many kingfishers to ignite
Halcyon thoughts?

I understand the reason for rainbows;
Dig deep where scattered light
Reforms into glistening treasure troves.
But does the singing of shallowing waves
Resolve unreasoned foreboding,
And shining sea-circles herald
The unloading of unkempt worries?
Do sunbeams point towards
A hub of transforming brightening
And clustering clouds confirm
The reality of silver linings?

Home Coming

A lodestone in the heart
Leads swallows
To a swirling conclusion
Of a lamb-bleating
Leaf-bursting homecoming.

A lodestone in the heart
Hides warblers
In blue-scented
Windflower-whitened woods
As ghost songs of spring.

A lodestone in the heart
Spins, and aches
For moments, places,
Real or imagined,
When the stone was still.

Waiting

It is a spring made reluctant
By a chillness on the wind;
Caution whispers from the east and north,
The greening made tentative
By winter's insensitive tenacity.
There is inertia deep in the earth,
Even the dark deer stand hesitant
In a wreck of woodland remnants;
How uncertain it all is.

It is a spring made melancholy
By the folly of flowers;
A faded umber pervades,
The yellow and gold tarnished
For want of the sun's varnish.
Renewal is delayed,
Even the brightness of blackthorn
Is blighted and forlorn;
How uneasy seem the optimists.

It is a spring made expectant
By dream-chants at dawn;
Songs of beginnings at first light,
Made hopeful of redemption
By pastel perceptions,
A subtle palate of blue, pink and white;
Small signs that herald a brightening,
Then a sighing and a scenting
And it all can start afresh.

Caution whispers from the east and north,
There is inertia deep in the earth,
How uncertain it all is.
A faded umber pervades,
Renewal is delayed,
How uneasy seem the optimists;
Songs of beginnings at first light,
A subtle palate of blue, pink and white
And it all can start afresh.

Old May Day

Make me a promise
By the hawthorn tree,
We will linger in its magic shade
If you will marry me.

Hedgerows wear
White ribbons
Marking boundaries
Between pasture and crops,
Between spring and summer.
Make me a walking-stick
Of stout quick-thorn,
So I can cross the valley's slopes
To bless the flocks and corn.

Shepherdless sheep
Wander hillside seclusion,
Then, in fleece-shone,
Writhe-rooted, fairy haunts
Find sanctuary.
Make me a blessing
When the moonflower blooms
To quell the fear of baleful Shades
By sanctifying gloom.

Maytime bleaches,
And suffuses
Sky-fragments of speedwell
And a sun-dust of cowslips
With foetid sweetness.
Make me a garland
And a may tree crown,
So I can sing the summer in
And dance the maypole round.

Glow Worms

Sparks from the
Grinding wheel
Spring sharp-bright;
For one or two nights
They smoulder,
Lonely incandescence
That never re-ignites
The past.

Shards from
Cascading meteors
Tangle in shadow webs;
For one or two nights
They smoulder,
Losing their light
In the dew
Of tomorrow morning.

Pinpricks in
The crust
Shine earth-beams;
For one or two nights
They smoulder,
Fitful sprites
Warning of turmoil
At the centre.

Winter Solstice

It should have been
A washed out day,
Colours drained and mixed
Into the turbidity of ditches.

It should have been
A raw day,
Warmth scoured by
Ice-toothed air.

It should have been
A troubled day,
Branches waved in
Desperate grieving.

It should have been
The darkest day,
A short interlude
Before the triumph of night.

It should have been
All these days
So that the turning point
Could be celebrated.

But it was an opal day,
A slack-tide day,
As the year
Tiptoed around winter.

Under Haven Brow

It is an unsettled place,
As the sea seeks
Its birthright
With patient endeavour,
Or fury unleashed
Against cathedral cliffs.

It is an unsettling place,
As unwritten histories
Shear away and dissolve
Assumed certainties
Into the bleached peripheries
Of a falling tide.

It is a fearful place,
As the maker unmakes
Its own creation,
And what is, will be
No more or less
Than transitory.

It is a saddening place,
Where sea lavender clings
For a little time,
While the wind flings
Profanity on the remnants
Of yesterday.

It is an indifferent place,
As we redeem
A shepherd's crown and
Armed with ancient magic,
Hope for a promised land
Rising from the sea.

EPILOGUE

We live in a world where change is inevitable, change at a human level such as how we live, how we work, how we communicate, what we know and aspire to and how our communities grow. There is also natural change, where the impact of the forces of wind, rain and tides and ecological dynamics mould our landscapes. However, we know that the way we manage the environment for food and other resources impacts on these natural processes of change and that this determines the make-up and quality of the natural and built environments.

We know the depth to which people have and could have influenced this part of the world in the past. But we cannot be certain how our current actions will affect it in the future, in particular how the process of climate change will impact on coastal erosion and flooding.

Nature will continue to create and cope with its own natural processes, but it is vital that we think clearly to ensure that our actions contribute to the benefit of the people, the wild plants and animals that together create the vibrancy and beauty of this exceptional area.

BIBLIOGRAPHY

ODHAM, John.   The Seaford Story.   SB Publication 1999
McCARTHY, E & M.   The Cuckmere. The Lindel Publishing Co 1981
LONGSTAFF-TYRRELL, Peter.   Reflections from the Cuckmere Valley.   Gote House Publishing Co 2004
LARKIN, Monty.   Seven Sisters. Ulmus Books 2008
JOHNSON, W.H.   Early Victorian Alfriston. Downsway Books 1993
CLARKE, Juliet.   Mr Russell's Little Floral Kingdom. Kingdom Books 1999
MATTHEWS, Mike.   Captain Swing in Sussex and Kent. The Hastings Press 2006
BRANDON, Peter.   The South Downs. Phillimore & Co Ltd 1998
WILLS, Barclay.   Edit. Payne and Pailthorpe.   The Downland Shepherds. Alan Sutton Publishing 1989
THE TRAMP.   The South Downs.   London, Brighton & South Coast Railway   (no date)
MacDERMOTT, Rev. K.H.   Sussex Church Music in the Past. Moore and Wingham 1922
STRONG, Roy.   A Little History of the English Country Church. Jonathon Cape 2007
BRAGG, Melvyn. The Adventure of English.   Hodder and Stoughton 2003
ROUD, Steve.   The English Year. Penguin Reference 2006
GRIGSON, Geoffrey.   The Englishman's Flora. Paladin 1975
MAYBEY, Richard.   Flora Britannica. Sinclair-Stevenson 1996
COCKER, Mark.   Birds Britannica. Chatto and Windus 2005
SHRUBB, Mike.   The Birds of Sussex. Phillimore & Co Ltd 1979
JAMES, Paul (Edit).   Birds of Sussex. Sussex Ornithological Society 1996
CAVENDISH, Richard.   Kings and Queens. The Concise Guide.   David and Charles 2007

Other Sources

Visitor Guides to Churches
Extracts from various editions of The Sussex Archaeological Review
Leaflets and archive information from Seaford Museum and Heritage Society
Leaflets from the Seven Sisters Country Park Visitor Centre

Contacts:

The Sussex Archaeological Society, Barbican House, 169 High Street, Lewes, East Sussex BN7 1YE
www.sussexpast.co.uk
Tel: 01273 405737

Seaford Museum and Heritage Society, PO Box 2132, The Esplanade, Seaford, East Sussex BN25 9BH
www.seafordmuseum.org.uk
Tel: 01323 898222

South Downs Society, 2 Swan Court, Station Road, Pulborough, West Sussex RH20 1RL
www.southdownssociety.org.uk
Tel: 01798 873108

Sussex Ornithological Society
www.sos.org.uk